Dedicated to Maxim 'Mo

written By Julie Zamora

illustrated by Berna rode

Kinderbutterflybooks.com
Copyright © 2021 Julie Zamora
Edited by: Bryan Palmer and Stephanie Cullen

"Max, it's time to get up!"
Mom shouts down the hall.

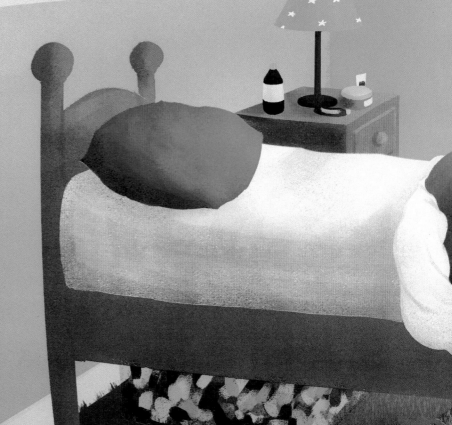

I go from laying down in my bed,
to standing up strong and tall
as I pick up my head.

My name is Maxim,
but Mom calls me Max

I prefer to use Patches,
and those are the facts!

Some superheroes have special powers like super strength,

but my super power is the pain that I can take!

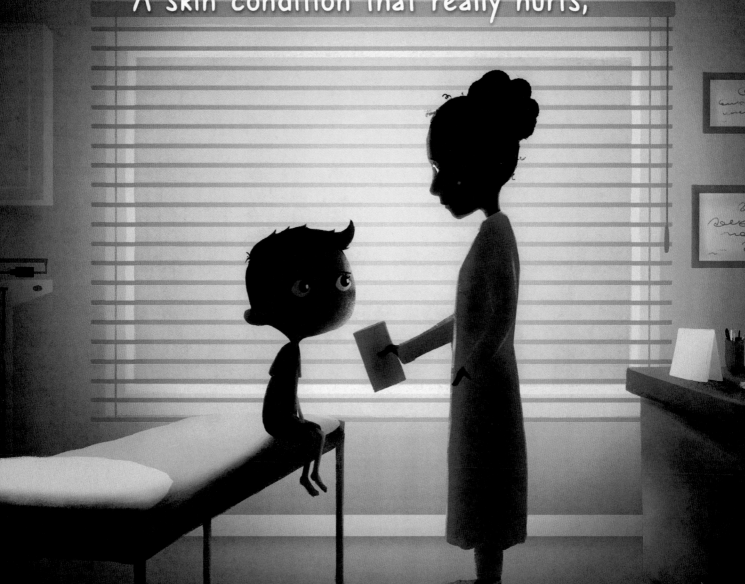

"You have eczema," the Doctor said.
A skin condition that really hurts,

it leaves my skin itchy, scratchy, red and ashy.

From my head to my toes,
on my arms and elbows,
are just a few places my rash shows.

It's even behind my legs,
ankles, and knees.
Oh, how I wish it would leave...
PLEASE!

All these places
cause itches
and scratches

which covers my body
with red, ashy rashes;

that's why I like to be called
Patches.

I like the name

Patches.

It makes me unique!

It's my superhero patch,
I like to think!

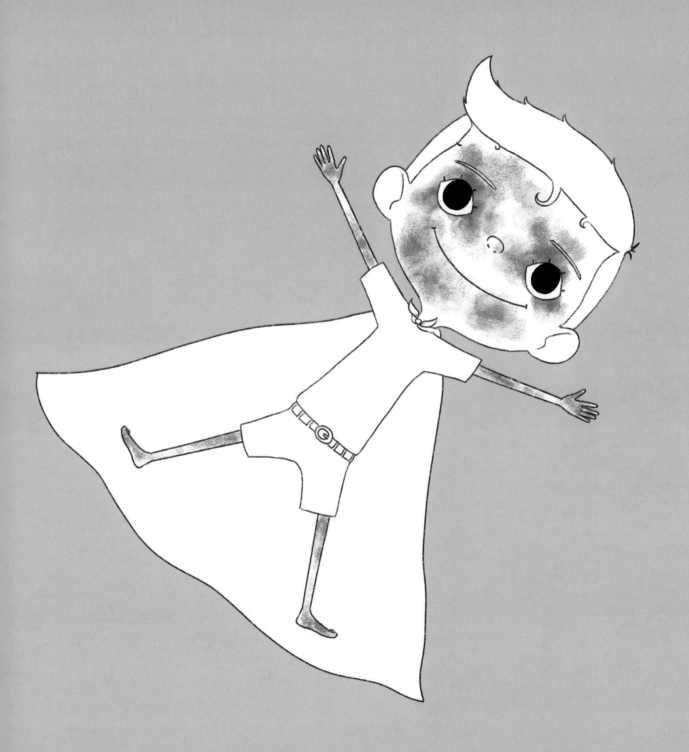

My friends don't understand my condition; you see...
They only know that my skin itches me.

When I play in the grass or swim in the pool,
the sun and my sweat leaves me in pain and regret.

We are all unique in our own special way,
so it's important to support one another
each and every day.

If you have eczema

- especially as much as me-

just know you are not alone,

and a team we can be!

I am lovable and huggable, and I want to save the day.

"Patches"
Pablo Picasso
Oil on canvas

I am like a rare painting from Picasso or Monet.

How boring would It be if we all looked the same?
You would look like me but
we would have different names.

Look in the mirror and be proud of what you see,
the world needs more art pieces like you and me.

Sometimes at night, I put up a fight,

because all of these medications and creams
really irritate me.

My skin is red
and has lots of rashes,

but I am a superhero,
and sometimes we get scratches.

My skin is not smooth, or pretty, or soft.
It's like snakeskin, and sometimes it even peels off.
Sometimes I bleed and scab up really bad, and people
will look and think, "OH MY GOSH, he's gone mad!"

Try not to judge until you
have walked in one's shoes...
did I mention I can't even wear my own shoes!

My eczema isn't contagious; you cannot catch it.

I just look a little different,
and I like to be called *Patches!*

Why can't my powers heal all of my scratches?

Not even the best baseball players
make all their catches.

To all of the children that have struggles like me, try to remember the superhero you can be.

Now put on your cape, your smile, and clothes, and go conquer the day because we are all SUPERHEROS!

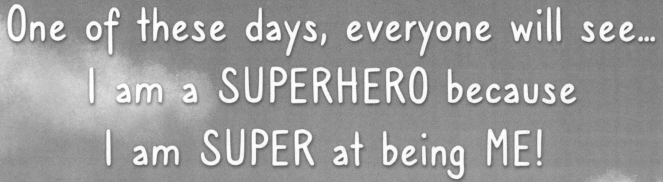

One of these days, everyone will see...
I am a SUPERHERO because
I am SUPER at being ME!

Made in the USA
Coppell, TX
17 November 2021

65934905R00019